Benny Learns to Say Goodbye

Kids and Parents Beating Fear of Separation

Written by
Dr. Jonathan Kushnir & Ram Kushnir

Illustrations
Vidya Lalgudi Jaishankar

Benny Learns to Say Goodbye
Kids and Parents Beating Fear of Separation

By: Dr. Jonathan Kushnir, Ram Kushnir

Printed in the United States of America

First Printing, 2022

ISBN: 9798355434229
Please visit us online for more information.

Facebook: https://www.facebook.com/groups/cbtails

Introduction for the Reading Parent

Separation from parents occurs naturally in a child's life. For example, going to kindergarten, school, visiting a friend or relative, or even going to the bathroom, are all activities that require separation. Children's ability to feel secure while away from their parents begins at an early age and is a significant developmental milestone.

Most children can confidently separate from their parents by the age of 5. However, this separation is very challenging for others, and each parting becomes a significant and stressful event for the child and their parents.

Children that are anxious about separation can feel very distressed. They often believe something terrible will happen to them or their parents, and they'll be left alone in the world. They cannot feel safe unless they are in the company of a parent. They avoid being apart from their caretakers. This behavior may negatively impact both parents and children. Children may avoid many social interactions and activities if one of their parents is not nearby. Parents, for their part, are often forced to stay with their children to reduce their level of distress. Therefore limiting their ability to conduct daily routines and enjoyable activities.

This book's intended to help parents and children overcome the fear of separation calmly and consciously. The story incorporates the principles of cognitive behavior therapy for dealing with these difficulties. It offers a gentle and straightforward way of coping with separation anxiety. In addition, throughout the book, you'll find explanations for parents, which describe the therapeutic principles utilized in the story and offer insightful information that connects the story to real life.

Enjoy reading!

Please note that this book is not a substitute for treatment by a qualified professional.

Once upon a time, there was a lion cub.
An adorable lion cub named Benny.
Benny lived with his family in Africa,
in a place where the plains are green
and wide, the sun shines warm,
and the animals run wild.

Benny had a great time in his African home.
What he loved most was being with his parents.
He explored the hills and the valleys with Dad,
and made colorful art with Mom.

In fact, he loved being close to
his parents so much, it was almost
impossible for him to say goodbye,
even for a moment.

6

When his parents were out of sight,

he was always sure something would happen.

Scary thoughts went through his head.

Thoughts like, "Did something happen to Mom and Dad?

Are they gone for good?

Who will protect me?

How will I find food?!"

Benny would also have unpleasant feelings in his body.
His heart pounded, his belly ached,
and he would sweat and sometimes shake.
Everywhere he went, even to bed or the bathroom,
he had to be sure his parents were still ok
and hadn't gone away.

For the parents

Various sensations may be felt as part of the normal
physiological response to a threatening situation and
preparing to deal with it. For example, accelerated pulse,
sweating, and rapid breathing.
These sensations typically decline and disappear as the
sense of threat passes.

"Daddy! Mommy! Are you there?"
He would ask again and again...
And although it sometimes made them angry,
they always replied, "It's alright, dear.
Do not be afraid. We're right here."

For the parents

Anxious kids repeatedly ask for reassurance by making sure
their parents are healthy and close by. Providing this constant
reassurance can worsen anxiety because it reinforces the idea
that the child cannot cope with it themselves.

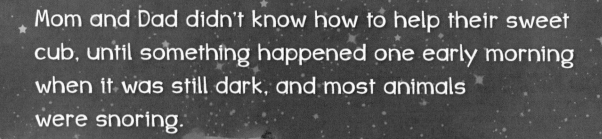

Mom and Dad didn't know how to help their sweet cub, until something happened one early morning when it was still dark, and most animals were snoring.

It was the morning of the journey to Tooth mountain. Every year, after the first rainfall, all of the lion cubs got up before dawn, climbed up Tooth mountain without their parents, and watched the sunrise together.

"I can't go," Benny said in a trembling voice.
"If something bad happens.
I'll be there all by myself,
while you're here, too far to help."
Mom smiled, "Do not worry, sweet boy.
If anything happens, we'll come at once."
Benny insisted, "What if something happens
to you when I'm gone? I'll be left all alone!"

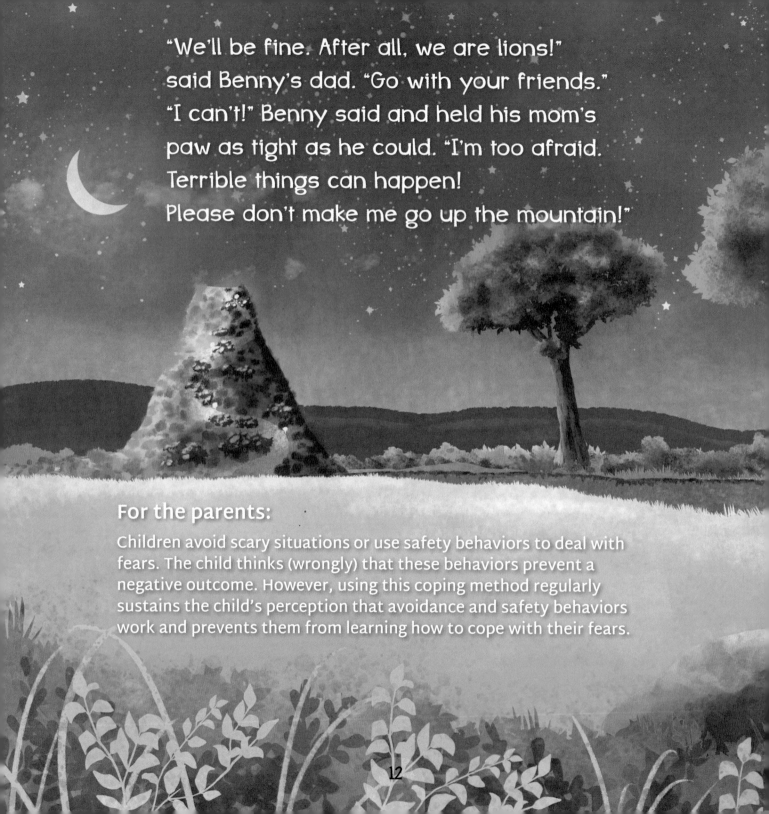

"We'll be fine. After all, we are lions!"
said Benny's dad. "Go with your friends."
"I can't!" Benny said and held his mom's
paw as tight as he could. "I'm too afraid.
Terrible things can happen!
Please don't make me go up the mountain!"

For the parents:

Children avoid scary situations or use safety behaviors to deal with fears. The child thinks (wrongly) that these behaviors prevent a negative outcome. However, using this coping method regularly sustains the child's perception that avoidance and safety behaviors work and prevents them from learning how to cope with their fears.

Benny's parents were helpless.
Their son was determined not to go.
As the lion family turned to go home,
they heard a familiar voice, "Hellooo lions!"
That was Agnes's voice. Agnes was an old lioness
whose wisdom was known all over the valley.

"I see little Benny cannot say goodbye!" Agnes said.
"Yes," Mom answered. "He won't be without us.
Even for a minute. "I see..." Agnes said while
Benny held his mother's paw tightly.
Dad added, "Benny really wants to say goodbye,
but he just can't, and we don't know
how to help him. We are all so frustrated!"

14

Agnes listened patiently and said,
"I think I know how to help. When I was little,
I, too, could not say goodbye to my parents."
"You did!?" Benny asked in surprise.
"Yes. I couldn't leave them for a second until
I overcame my frightening thoughts." Agnes said.
"You had frightening thoughts?" Benny asked.

Agnes replied, "Yes. You see, sometimes frightening thoughts pop into our heads. Thoughts that are untrue and phony. It is as if someone's sitting in our heads, like a big bully, making up these scary stories.

"What can we do about that bully?" Dad asked. "Let's start by giving him a name," Agnes said. "What name would you like to give him?" She asked Benny.

"Can I pick any name I want?"

"Of course."

"Then I would like to name him... *Fakey*"

"That's a great name," said Agnes.

"He really does tell fake stories!"

For the parents:

The concept Agnes shows here is called externalization. She is naming the scary process to distinguish between the child's frightening thoughts and the child themself. Referring to fear as an external entity helps the child treat it as something they can and must deal with. You can choose all kinds of names, for example, The Bully, Grumpy, Goofy, Tricksy, etc.

"And to get rid of Fakey, we'll need to take small steps. One after another," Agnes said. "With each little step, you will learn to be less and less with Mom and Dad." Benny nodded. "Now, look over there." Agnes pointed to a tall tree.

18

This tree started out as a little seed,
It grew and became a sprout,
then it grew a little more into a young tree,
and then it developed thick branches,
and continued growing until it became
tall and magnificent."

"I get it," Benny said.
"The little seed had to go through
all the steps before it became a tree."
"Exactly, smart cub," Agnes said.
"And you can do it too! Now, back to Fakey.
I have some tasks for you."

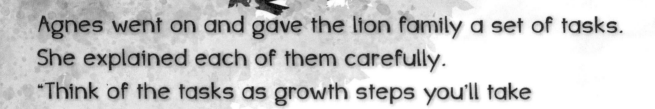

Agnes went on and gave the lion family a set of tasks.
She explained each of them carefully.
"Think of the tasks as growth steps you'll take
on your way to the sky. Same as our tree."

"And I'm warning you, Fakey will have
a few things to say, to try to make you
go the wrong way. But whatever he says,
they are just *stories!* "
"Thank you, Agnes!" said the lion family
as they turned back home.

Benny was relieved he stayed with Mom
and Dad that day, but in his heart, he wished
he could be like the other cubs and say goodbye
to his parents.
He was super excited about Agnes's plan.

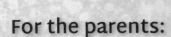

For the parents:

Like any coping process, overcoming fear has to be done gradually, in small doses -
in steps that the child can deal with despite their fears. Slowly and gradually, after
a certain degree of security has been achieved, we can increase the difficulty level.
Persistence is essential here. To help formalize the process, you can define milestones
or levels. You can do that together with the child. Indicate the task the child should
complete at each level, and after every success, you can mark the job as completed in
any creative way you see fit.

The next day, Mom said to Benny,
"It's time for our first task." They stood
near a tall Baobab tree, and Mom said,
"Benny, stand with your back to me
and I will begin to walk away."

"As I walk further from the tree,
you will stop hearing my footsteps.
Your job is to hold off your fear and concern
and stay without me until I return."
"OK, let's do it," Benny said,
although he was scared.

22

Mom walked away until her footsteps
faded in the distance. Benny began
feeling hot and sweaty. Pretty soon,
bad thoughts popped into his head.
And just when he was about to call Mom,
he heard her voice, "Well done, my boy!"
Mom was standing next to Benny, and
he immediately felt better.

For the parents:

The first and easiest exercise you can do with your child is the same as shown
here. Let the child stay without you in a controlled environment for increasing
periods. You can do this exercise over days and keep track of the period the
child succeeded in staying by themselves.

"OK, let's try again. This time I'll go
for a longer time," Mom said.
"I'm ready," Benny replied.
Mom's steps quietened as she walked away.
Benny held out nicely until, after a few moments,
he heard a distant animal growl.

"Something happened to Mom!" He immediately thought. Benny's heart pounded heavily, but he tried his best to stay calm. He managed to hold himself for another few moments until he called,

"Mom! Where are you??! Come back!"

Mom quickly returned and stood beside him.
"I'm here, sweety." She said,
Benny was super relieved to see her.
"That's enough practice for today."
Mom said. "You did great. Tomorrow we'll
give it another go. It will be easier. I know"

In the next few days, Benny continued practicing being away from Mom for longer and longer times, He became good at it and could stay calm even if he heard frightening noises. He also noticed that Fakey and his stories were quieter. "Great Job Benny!" Mom and Dad said, "But we still have work to do."

"It's time for your next step," Dad said the next morning. "From now on, Mom and I will be less and less by your side when you go to bed and bathroom.
"Are you sure I can stand that?" Benny asked in a worried voice.
"Of course you can! We'll do it in small steps, just like Agnes said."

And for the following days,
when Benny went to the bathroom,
instead of standing where he could see them,
Benny's parents let him go by himself
and once, in a while called, "Yoo-Hoo! We're here."

For the parents:

Like in the previous exercise, the idea here is to let the child stay in anxiety-inducing states for increasingly longer periods. In this exercise, the parent reduces their presence by calling to the child periodically instead of being in eye contact the entire time.

Each time he went to the bathroom,
they let him be alone for longer times.
They continued to do that until he
spent the whole time in the bathroom
all by himself, without a single "Yoo,"
nor a "Hoo" nor a "Hey!"

Benny started to get the hang of it,
and Fakey's stories weakened.
When Benny went to bed, his parents
didn't stay with him until he fell asleep.
Instead, they visited his bed every
few minutes. Each day they let him
be alone for longer and longer times.

After a few days, Benny got really good
at going to bed by himself as well.
"Keep going, Benny. You're doing great!"
His parents said to their courageous cub.

"I think it's time for your next task,"
Mom said. "Today, I will take you to
a friend and leave you two to play alone.
I'll be gone for a very short time."

Benny never stayed at a friend's
without his parents. "What if something
happens when you're gone?" He asked.
"Hey, isn't that Fakey talking? You will do great,
just like you did so far." Mom said and smiled.
"It is Fakey!" Benny realized and smiled
back, ready for the next task.

Mom and Benny went to visit Benny's friend, William the rhino. They arrived at William's, and Mom let the two kids play for a while. Then she said to Benny, "I am leaving you two alone. I'll return later as I promised." Benny overcame his fear and gave his mother a kiss goodbye.

William and Benny played together and Benny held nicely. That went on until thoughts began popping into his head, "Is Mom OK? Shouldn't she be back by now?" Then he realized something, "These thoughts are Fakey's stories!" And he continued to play, trying to stay calm.

But as time passed, Benny's concerns grew deeper and deeper until he couldn't hold it any longer and told William, "I have to see my mom NOW!" "Don't worry, Benny. She'll be here shortly." William said. But Benny couldn't wait any longer, and he burst into tears.

As Benny cried, he suddenly saw
Mom standing in front of the two boys.
Benny ran to Mom and held her
as tight as he could.

That evening Benny talked with his parents.
"I don't think I can do it. It's too hard!"
"Sure you can! You simply need to practice."
Dad said. "We're taking it step-by-step. Remember,
your fears are made of Fakey's stories. That's all."
Benny felt Better and decided not to give up.

For the parents:

Throughout the process, there can be ups and downs. Parents
must continue to reassure and encourage the child to keep
coping, despite their fears.

The next day, Dad took Benny to visit William again. When they arrived, Dad told Benny, "I will be back in a short while. You can do it, sweet boy!"
Benny took two deep breaths and said to himself, "I will not let Fakey take over today." "Go away, stories!" He roared in confidence.

For the parents:

Children use self-talk to help themselves cope with fear. For example, "I won't let fear beat me. It's scary at first, but if I don't give up, my fears will disappear."

40

The boys played with William's wooden figures.
After some time, Benny began feeling uncomfortable,
but he stayed calm. Suddenly, he heard
a familiar voice, "You boys are playing so nice!"
It was Dad. He was back, and Benny
was surprised at how quickly it seemed.

That evening Benny was thrilled.
"I managed to stay without mom and
dad today!" he thought while lying in bed.
His heart pounded. This time with excitement.

Over the next few days, Mom and Dad
kept leaving Benny with William and other
friends for longer and longer times.
With each day of practice, Benny felt
more comfortable staying without his parents.

For the parents:

Through the gradual process, Benny's confidence grew, and he could stay
alone without his parents for longer periods.

Mom and Dad continued to make
sure Benny stayed without them
as much as they could,
and each day, Fakey got quieter
while Benny's confidence grew.

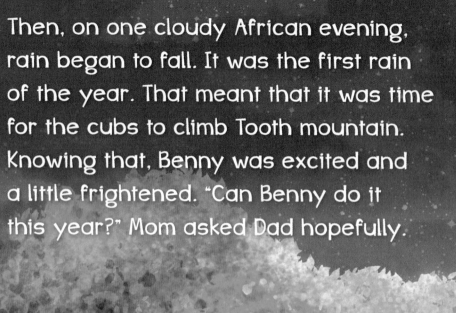

Then, on one cloudy African evening,
rain began to fall. It was the first rain
of the year. That meant that it was time
for the cubs to climb Tooth mountain.
Knowing that, Benny was excited and
a little frightened. "Can Benny do it
this year?" Mom asked Dad hopefully.

Just before dawn, the cubs and their
parents met at the feet of the mountain.
Benny saw the other cubs gather.
He looked at his parents, took two deep breaths,
and said, "Goodbye, Mom and Dad,
I will see you when I return."
And he joined the other cubs

From the top of the mountain, Benny
took a long view of the sun rising
over the African plains. It was breathtaking.
Benny felt as happy and free as
he ever did, while back home,
Mom and Dad were the proudest
parents in Africa.

Oh, one more thing...
Sometimes Fakey still tries to put stories
into Benny's head, but Benny reminds himself
that they are just stories, and although
being with Mom and Dad is still what
Benny loves most, he can say goodbye
whenever he wants.

For the parents:

We must remember that the fears do not disappear completely.
We need to encourage our children to go on and improve their
coping ability all the time as challenging situations continue to occur.

Dr. Kushnir

Clinical Psychologist

Dr. Jonathan Kushnir is a clinical psychologist, an expert and an instructor in Cognitive Behavior Therapy, accredited by the European Association for Behavioral Therapies.

After completing his Ph.D. in clinical psychology in Israel and a research fellowship in the U.S, he has successfully treated thousands of children and adults suffering from emotional anxieties for over a decade. His insightful articles on the subject have been published in top scientific - peer-reviewed journals.

This book is part of the *CBT tails* series, which makes CBT principles accessible and clear to kids and parents.

"The idea for the *CBT tails* series was born after treating numerous children and their parents and observing their rough and frustrating struggles with anxiety, anger, and sleep disorders.

In this book, we aim to deliver the knowledge accumulated over the years in a unique and straightforward way; one that can be easily understood by kids and adults alike."

If you enjoyed our book, it would be great if you left a review to let others know that they, too, can benefit from this book.

Your review will also help us see what is and isn't working so we can better serve all our readers.

Scan to add a review:

Made in the USA
Las Vegas, NV
08 February 2024

85507712R00031